The Red Army of the Great Patriotic War 1941–45

Steven J Zaloga · Illustrated by Ron V...

Series editor Martin Windrow

First published in Great Britain in 1984 by
Osprey Publishing, Elms Court, Chapel Way,
Botley, Oxford OX2 9LP, United Kingdom.
Email: info@ospreypublishing.com

British Library Cataloguing in Publication Data

Zaloga, Steven J.
  The Soviet army 1941–45.—(Men-at-arms: 216)
  1. Union of Soviet socialist Republic. Army
History-Bibliography
  I. Title   II. Series
  355′.00947

  ISBN 0-85045-939-7

Filmset in Great Britain
Printed in China through World Print Ltd.
Series Editor: MARTIN WINDROW

FOR A CATALOGUE OF ALL BOOKS PUBLISHED BY
OSPREY MILITARY AND AVIATION PLEASE CONTACT:

The Marketing Manager, Osprey Direct UK,
PO Box 140, Wellingborough, Northants,
NN8 4ZA, United Kingdom.
Email: info@ospreydirect.co.uk

The Marketing Manager, Osprey Direct USA,
c/o Motorbooks International, PO Box 1, Osceola,
WI 54020-0001, USA.
Email: info@ospreydirectusa.com

www.ospreypublishing.com

Artist's note

Readers may care to note that the original paintings
from which the colour plates in this book were
prepared are available for private sale. All
reproduction copyright whatsoever is retained by the
Publishers. All enquiries should be addressed to:
  Model Emporium
  700 North Johnson,
  Suite N, El Cajon
  California 92020
  USA
The Publishers regret that they can enter into no
correspondence upon this matter.

The Red Army of the Great Patriotic War 1941-5

The Red Army in 1941

On the verge of war in the summer of 1941, the Red Army[1] was the largest in the world; but its enormous size could not disguise its serious weaknesses. It had performed well against Japan in the Far East at Khalkin Gol in 1939, but its performance during its unopposed invasion of eastern Poland in September 1939 was lacklustre. It gave the Germans the impression of an army ill-suited to modern, mechanised warfare. This impression proved all too accurate in the winter of 1939–1940, when the Soviet Union tried to bully its tiny neighbour, Finland, into unilateral territorial concessions. The small Finnish army humiliated

[1] The Red Army was officially called the RKKA: Rabochiy Krestyanskaya Krasnaya Armiya (Red Army of Workers and Peasants) until 1946 when it was renamed the Soviet Army.

the Soviets in one of the most embarrassing fiascos of 20th century warfare. The Russo-Finnish War whetted Hitler's appetite for invasion.

The sorry state of the Red Army was mostly due to Stalin's political repression. The Red Army had been decapitated in the purges of the late 1930s. It was not only the large number of officers killed that proved so devastating: it was the quality of the victims. The cowed remnants proved ill-suited to

A rifle battalion commander consults with one of his company commanders during the fighting in September 1941. The officer to the left is a captain, as is evident from the single rectangle on the collar tab. The Rifle Forces emblem is also seen on the tab. Interestingly enough, the tab appears to be the subdued wartime style, even though he wears the pre-war red and gold rank chevron on his sleeve. The lieutenant to the right has the two square pips of his rank on his collar, but notice that there is no evidence of a tab. Both officers are wearing the Model 1940 steel helmet, and the captain is armed with a PPD-40 sub-machine gun. (Sovfoto, as are all photographs not otherwise credited.)

prepare the Red Army for its greatest challenge. In the late 1930s, European armies were trying to develop the new skills of mechanised warfare. The Red Army had all the spanking new tools: tanks, trucks and radios. But the loss of most of the experienced and far-sighted leaders in the Great Purge, and continuing political interference and executions, undermined these efforts. It is worth noting that the units which successfully fought the Japanese in 1939 had escaped the worst ravages of the purges, while the units in Finland were more typical of Red Army units in Europe.

The most visible evidence of political interference was the *kommisar*. Each unit of battalion size and above had a kommisar in addition to the usual unit commander. It was a system of joint command introduced during the Civil War of 1917–21 to keep watch over professional officers, most of whom had served in the Tsar's army. The kommisar had to give his approval for any major order by the unit commander. Kommisars did not have any particular military skills, and were selected above all for their loyalty to the Communist Party. Many kommisars kept their noses out of military business and concentrated on their main tasks of political indoctrination, morale-building and training; but many used their post to intimidate loyal officers, and to interfere in military matters of which they had no experience. The situation was further exacerbated by the use of the *Komsomol* as an additional tool of the party during the purges. The Komsomol was a youth organisation that young soldiers could join before they reached the age to enter the Communist Party itself. Membership in the Komsomol during 1937–38 increased dramatically due to Party encouragement. Komsomol members in military units were expected to hold meetings during which officers and kommisars could be criticised and denounced. It became impossible to discipline soldiers in some units, since they would be provoked by the reproach to denounce the officer. Normal military discipline began to collapse, and severe demoralisation took place. In the wake of the Finland fiasco, reforms began to be instituted, including a reduction in the

A sapper removing a mine, September 1941. Many troops still retained the older Model 1936 helmet. The foreground man is armed with a Tokarev SVT-38 automatic rifle while the sappers behind have Moisin rifles. Note the absence of identifiable rank insignia. The gasmask bag is the later type with side compartments, for the BN gasmask.

rôle of the kommisar in August 1940. But the damage was too extensive to repair in the few months that remained before the German invasion. The Red Army was plagued by a lack of experienced officers; leadership was too often in the hands of incompetents, timid men who had been cowed into submission, and boot-licking opportunists.

The German invasion on Sunday, 22 June 1941 led to a series of staggering defeats and catastrophic losses. In the five months of fighting in 1941 the Soviets lost about four million men (more than a million dead, and the rest POWs). This was 80 per cent of the total strength of the ground forces at the time of the outbreak of the war, and would amount to nearly 60 per cent of the military losses suffered by the Soviet Union in the whole four years of war. Armoured vehicle losses were close to 20,000— about six times larger than the total size of the attacking German armour force. Some units fought with tenacity and incredible bravery, like the garrison of the Brest fortress; but many others folded up without a serious fight and surrendered.

A Red Army patrol, September 1941. The nearest rifleman is armed with the PPD-40 sub-machine gun, while the soldiers behind carry Tokarev SVT-38s. Note that the nearest rifleman wears the old Tsarist leather cartridge pouch on his back. All are wearing the Model 1940 steel helmet.

The criminally abusive treatment meted out by the Communist Party did little to engender loyalty to the Soviet state amongst the rank and file of Soviet soldiers.

Yet the Red Army managed to hold on. There were many fine young officers, too junior to have attracted Stalin's malevolent attention. Within a few months Russian attitudes began to harden. The fighting was no longer viewed as a defence of the Party, but a defence of the Russian homeland. Not surprisingly, the war is known as the Great Patriotic War to Soviet citizens. Reserves were called up, and by the end of 1941 the Red Army had been rebuilt to a strength equal to about half the divisions available at the outset of the war. The German Wehrmacht had finally overstretched its capabilities, and in bitter fighting on the approaches to Moscow it was finally stopped. Young officers were catapulted into regimental and

The heavy weapons company of a rifle battalion mount up on a GAZ-AA truck. The soldier to the left is carrying a 50-PM 38 mortar. Two soldiers near the truck are loading a 7.62mm Maxim Model 1910 machine gun aboard, on its characteristic wheeled mounting.

divisional commands far beyond their experience. Many proved incapable, and as often as not died on the battlefield with their men. Many others learned the art of command under the most appalling of circumstances, and helped lead the Red Army to victory after four bloody years of war.

The Germans retained the strategic initiative the following summer, ranging deep into the Ukraine and Caucasus in a drive for the Soviet oilfields. The summer of 1942 was very costly for the Red Army, with several catastrophic encirclements all too reminiscent of the débâcles of 1941. But the Soviets were gradually learning their lessons. In the summer of 1942 they began deploying large armoured formations, the tank and mechanised corps. At first these were handled amateurishly. Experience and tactical skill in modern warfare came at a horrible price. But the skills were learned, as displayed most dramatically at Stalingrad in the winter of 1942–43. Stalingrad represented the high

water mark of the German invasion. Although it is often called the turning point of the war in the East, the Germans in fact retained the strategic initiative until the summer of 1943; it was the battle of the Kursk salient in June–July 1943 that marked the real turning point. Not only was the German offensive decisively smashed, but Soviet forces went over to the offensive on a strategic level, and would never again be seriously checked by the Germans.

Western views of the Great Patriotic War tend to be coloured by clichés and myths popularised by German generals in their books from the 1950s. The Red Army is seen as a great, plodding force relying on mass rather than tactical skill. At the small unit level, the Red Army was not particularly impressive; Soviet infantry platoons and companies were far more poorly trained than their German counterparts. Nevertheless, the gap in tactical skill between the Germans and Soviets narrowed as the war dragged on. The Germans were hard-pressed to fill out their units, and by 1943–44, their own small unit training declined. At higher command levels the Soviets began outpacing the Germans by the end of 1943. In the operational arts, the Soviet generals managed to bluff, baffle and overwhelm their German opponents. The débâcle in Byelorussia in the summer of 1944, which saw the complete rout of the German Army Group Centre, was the best evidence of the growing skill of the Red Army's commanders.

Organisation of the Soviet Armed Forces: The Rifle Forces

At the outbreak of the war, the Soviet Armed Forces consisted of five main elements: the Ground Forces, Navy, Air Force, National Air Defence and Armed Forces Support. The Ground Forces were the largest element by far, amounting to 79.3 per cent, the Air Force 11.5 per cent and the Navy only 5.8 per cent. The Ground Forces were broken up into five main combat arms, as well as a number of technical and support elements. The main combat arms were the Rifle Forces, Tank and Mechanised Forces, Artillery, Cavalry and Air Assault Forces. The smaller technical branches included the railroad, automotive, engineer, chemical defence, and signals forces.

*　　*　　*

The Soviets referred to their infantry branch as Rifle Forces, reflecting an old Russian tradition that viewed riflemen (*streltsi*) as more élite than mere infantry (*pyekhoty*). The Rifle Forces were the largest single element of the Red Army during the war, amounting to 75 per cent of its line divisions. At the outbreak of the war the Red Army had 303 divisions, of which 88 were in the process of formation and not entirely combat ready. There were four principal types of rifle divisions at the time: the basic rifle divisions (178), mountain rifle divisions (18), motor rifle divisions for the mechanised corps (31) and independent motorised rifle divisions (two).

In the summer of 1941 the rifle division was in a state of reorganisation after the débâcle in Finland. Under the new April 1941 orders, the division numbered 14,483 men based around three infantry

A woman military correspondent interviews a rifle unit going to the front. Correspondents were attached to the army's political administration, so she is wearing the sleeve star insignia and black-edged collar tab normally worn by *kommisars* and *politruks*. The soldier in the peaked cap is a senior sergeant, evident from the three triangles on his collar tabs.

regiments. Fire support came from two artillery regiments, an anti-tank and an anti-aircraft battalion. Tank support was very modest—only 16 light tanks—as most of the tanks were being hoarded in the new mechanised corps. The June 1941 invasion caught the Red Army in the middle of the reorganisation, and most infantry formations were based on older tables. The summer 1941 fighting was horribly costly, with over 100 rifle divisions destroyed.

The war led to the immediate call-up of all 23–36-year-old males, the 18–22-year-olds having already been inducted before the outbreak of war. By July 1941 some 5.3 million Soviets were under arms. The Red Army of 1941 was primarily Slavic: Russian, Ukrainian or Byelorussian. The Red Army did not recruit extensively from Central Asia,

Winter 1941: a colonel gives instruction on assaulting a strongpoint. His rank is most evident from the sleeve insignia three gold chevrons on a red background. Note the use of the *shapka-ushanka* fur winter cap by the officers. The rifleman to the left wears a civilian *ushanka*, while the one to the right is military issue.

the Caucasus or the Far East even though the non-Slavic minorities represented over a quarter of the Soviet population. The problem was mainly one of assimilating the non-Russian-speaking groups into the army. The exceptions to this were the mountain rifle divisions, which typically recruited Georgians and other peoples from the Caucasus, and cavalry divisions. This recruitment policy would change as the war dragged on.

Some idea of the horrendous losses suffered by the Red Army during this period can be gained from the fact that the Soviets raised 400 new divisions between the summer of 1941 and December 1941, but only had 80 divisions ready to field against the Germans at the end of that period. A total of 124 rifle divisions were erased from the records due to heavy losses, and some new formations were built around the skeletal remains

of old divisions, sometimes with only a few hundred survivors.

The enormous casualties suffered by the Red Army in the summer of 1941 led to a drastic reorganisation of the rifle divisions. The motor rifle divisions, intended to complement the tank divisions in the mechanised corps, had never been entirely formed. Many were wiped out, and the handful that survived until December 1941 were motorised in name only. They mostly disappeared through attrition. One independent motorised division, the 1st Moscow Motorised Rifle Division, was kept in service largely due to its fine performance. The basic rifle divisions were subjected to another reorganisation in July 1941, mainly due to the loss of equipment in the great encirclement battles. The pressing need for new formations led to their dilution in strength. A total of 286 new rifle divisions were formed between the outbreak of war and December 1941. Divisional strength fell from 14,483 to 10,859 men. The heaviest cut came in artillery, with divisional firepower suffering greatly as a result. Indeed, it was not until the winter of 1944–45 that Soviet rifle divisions began to be built up to pre-war levels in terms of available artillery support, relying instead on mortars.

The quality of Soviet infantry fell very rapidly. Training was minimal. Of the 286 new divisions, 24 were People's Volunteer Divisions, which were nothing more than elderly civilian volunteers with small arms. A further 22 divisions were formed by absorbing troops from other branches of the service, often with no infantry training. Nevertheless, they accomplished their purpose. By the winter of 1941–42 the front had been stabilised, and the Germans had been beaten back from the gates of Leningrad and Moscow.

The Slavic ethnic groups suffered most heavily from the enormous manpower losses of 1941–42. In addition, the German occupation of the western USSR covered much of the Ukraine and most of Byelorussia. As a result the Soviets were obliged to recruit more heavily amongst the ethnic minorities of the Caucasus, Central Asia and the Far East.

During the war the Red Army formed at least 42 'national' divisions and over 20 national brigades, composed of Lithuanians, Uzbekis, Armenians and other ethnic groups, generally commanded by Russian officers. The Baltic units served a political as well as military purpose, being intended to show local acceptance of Soviet rule after the annexation of the Baltic republics in 1940. In the Transcaucasus the reasons were primarily military, due to the fighting in the region in 1942. Details of these national divisions are unclear, since some were regular rifle divisions which happened to be raised in the regions, while others were specifically earmarked as ethnic formations. Divisions raised in the area included four Azeri, five Armenian, eight

Col. Aleksandr I. Lizyukov, commander of the highly decorated 1st Moscow Motorised Rifle Division, talking with tankers of the unit. Lizyukov commanded the 36th Tank Division in the summer of 1941; and after his successful leadership of the 1st Moscow Mot. Rifle Div. in the defence of Moscow he was given command of the 2nd Tank Corps, and eventually the 5th Tank Army. He was killed in action in July 1942. The tankers are wearing the *shuba* sheepskin coat, while the colonel wears the normal greatcoat. Barely evident are the subdued collar tabs on the greatcoat, with the four metal rectangles of a colonel.

A VDV brigade prepares for an airdrop during the 1942 Vyazma operation. The VDV units did not have any distinctive uniform, generally wearing a mixture of Red Army and Air Force gear. Here, they have ordinary winter snow coveralls over normal winter-issue Red Army uniforms.

Georgian and a number of mixed rifle divisions. (In Central Asia, the tradition of the Cossack cavalry led to the formation of cavalry divisions rather than infantry. This included five Uzbeki, three Tadzhik, three Kirkhiz, two Turkmen, 12 Kazakh, two Kalmyk, two Bakshir, one Checheno-Ingush and one Kabardino-Balkarian cavalry divisions.)

The Red Army also increased its intake of Russian women. Women had traditionally been recruited as doctors and medics, and at first filled non-combat support positions in rear areas. However, the situation became so bad that women were eventually allowed into the combat arms. Women were used in anti-aircraft units; and there are the celebrated cases of three combat air regiments with women crews. Women were also recruited as snipers, although they were not generally recruited into normal infantry units. In the last year of the war the ranks of tankers had become so depleted that women who worked at the tank plants, and who were familiar with driving and repairing tanks, were recruited as drivers. Many proved so able that they eventually rose to the command of their tank units. A total of 76 Russian women were awarded the highest Soviet military distinction, the 'Hero of the Soviet Union'. A third of these went to aircrew (27), and a third to partisans or resistance fighters (21). Eight women snipers, two scouts, one tanker and 12 medics also won the award, many posthumously. By the end of the war, about 10 per cent of the personnel of the Soviet armed forces were women, mainly Russians.

The Soviets also formed several allied armies in 1943. The Polish People's Army (LWP) was the largest of these, formed mainly from ex-prisoners of war and deportees. The LWP grew quite sizeable in 1944-45, when Poland was wrested from German control. For example, during the Berlin fighting Polish units made up nearly a tenth of the forces involved.[1] A Czechoslovak and a Yugoslav army were also formed, but they were very small owing to a lack of manpower. After the fall of Romania and Bulgaria these armies were allied to the Red Army, but they remained equipped and organised as before the switch in allegiance.

Equipment

The fighting in 1941 forced the Soviets to examine the equipment needs of the rifle forces. Soviet infantry equipment was based on both tactical needs and the restricted abilities of Soviet industry to provide equipment. One of the most obvious differences between the Red Army and the Wehrmacht was the relative balance of rifles to sub-machine guns. During the war the Soviet Union manufactured 18.3 million rifles and SMGs, of which 6.1 million (34 per cent) were sub-machine guns. In contrast, the Germans manufactured 11.6 million rifles and SMGs, of which only 1.2 million (11 per cent) were sub-machine guns. Indeed, by the end of the war, the popular image of the Red Army soldier was linked with the ubiquitous PPSh sub-machine gun.

Soviet preference for this type of infantry weapon stemmed from two causes. On the one hand, the PPSh and its close relatives were cheaper and easier to manufacture than normal rifles which require longer rifled barrels and precise machining. The PPSh used pistol ammunition, which was also cheaper than rifle ammunition as it consumed less propellant and brass. The other reason was related to training. Rifle fire, to be effective, requires training and practice—commodities that were in short supply in Russia during the war. In contrast, the PPSh required little marksmanship training, and was ideally suited to close-range skirmishing. German sub-machine guns like the MP40 were precision-crafted weapons. They were usually issued to section leaders or troops with special requirements; they were never issued as lavishly as

[1]See Men-at-Arms 117, *The Polish Army 1939–45*.

the Soviet SMGs, and many German infantrymen prized captured PPShs over the standard German 98k rifle. (It might also be noted that Russian troops, especially scouts, prized captured MP38s and MP40s for their compactness and light weight.)

Distribution of Soviet infantry weapons depended upon the type of infantry unit. The normal rifle company during the middle of the war had three rifle platoons and a machine gun platoon, with a total of three heavy Maxim water-cooled machine guns, nine DP light machine guns, 85 rifles or carbines, 12 SMGs and eight pistols. Officially, an infantry squad of nine men was armed with one SMG (the sergeant who led the squad), a DP squad machine gun, and seven rifles. Thus, in 1943, the normal Soviet rifle unit was actually not much different from its German equivalent, with very few sub-machine guns compared to rifles. Where the Soviets tended to concentrate their sub-machine guns was in the motor rifle units attached to tank and mechanised corps, or to independent tank brigades. A motor rifle company would have nine DP section machine guns, 27 rifles or carbines, 57 SMGs and five pistols. In a motor rifle section, the majority of the troops would be armed with automatic weapons.

The motor rifle units were the shock troops of the Rifle Forces. Despite their name, they had very few motor vehicles. They were usually carried into battle riding on tanks, a practice called *tankoviy desant* by the Russians. The Soviet motor rifle units were the equivalent of German Panzer Grenadier units. Another factor affecting the distribution of infantry weapons was the matter of Guards' status. The 'Guards' distinction was another throw-back to Tsarist practice. Units which won Guards status due to their combat performance were entitled to higher pay, better clothing and a better selection of equipment. This often meant that Guards rifle divisions were closer to the official tables of organisation as far as equipment was concerned when compared to less distinguished rifle units.

A section from an anti-tank rifle platoon in action in the Ukraine during the June 1942 fighting. The gunner is armed with a PTRS 14.5mm anti-tank rifle. The platoon leader, a senior sergeant, has a uniform distinctly darker in shade than the troops, probably the winter-issue wool rather than the summer issue cotton or linen worn by the privates. All the enlisted men carry their greatcoats bedroll fashion, and wear the *pilotka* sidecap. The riflemen in the background are armed with the popular PPSh sub-machine gun.

Senior Lieutenant Mikhalchenko, assistant chief of staff of a cavalry regiment in April 1942. He still wears the pre-war blue collar tabs and sleeve chevron. He is armed with a traditional *shashka*, Cossack sabre.

The distribution of weapons changed with time. At the beginning of the war Red Army rifle units had few if any SMGs. Officially, by the end of the war, even regular motor rifle units had a mixture of about one-third SMGs and two-thirds rifles and carbines. The accompanying charts show the shift in rifle division equipment through the war. However, few divisions in combat actually reached these levels.

One of the major drawbacks in Soviet infantry tactics was the lack of attention paid to infantry mechanisation. The Red Army was the only major European army not to adopt an armoured infantry carrier during the war. As mentioned earlier,

Soviet motor rifle troops usually went into action riding the tanks themselves—a risky substitute for infantry vehicles. German officers who served in Russia during the war singled out the lack of Soviet mechanised infantry as one of the main tactical failures of the Red Army during the war. The reasons for this appear to have more to do with production constraints than with tactical doctrine. The Soviets were hard-pressed to maintain tank production sufficient to replace combat attrition for most of the war. Production of armoured infantry vehicles would have cut into tank production, or some other vital aspect of weapons production. The Soviets viewed them as an unaffordable luxury during the war, though they began an extensive programme of infantry mechanisation after final victory.

The war on the Eastern Front was characterised by the heavy use of tank forces; and it was infantry units that were often victimised by tanks. The Soviets were much more backward in developing effective anti-tank weapons than any of the major European armies. In 1941 they began adding anti-tank rifle units to their formations; a rifle battalion received an anti-tank rifle platoon with six PTRD or PTRS rifles, and a motor rifle regiment had an anti-tank rifle company added, usually with 24 rifles. These weapons were suitable against the lightly armoured tanks of 1941–42; but due to the rapid escalation in tank armour forced on the Germans by the T-34, by the end of 1942 these guns

	April 1941	July 1941	December 1941	July 1942	July 1943	December 1944
Red Army Rifle Divisions 1941–45: Tables of Equipment						
Troops	14,483	10,859	11,626	10,386	9,380	11,706
Horses	3,000	2,500	2,400	1,800	1,700	1,200
Trucks	558	203	248	149	124	342
Rifles	10,420	8,341	8,565	7,241	6,274	6,330
SMG	1,204	171	582	711	1,048	3,594
LMG	392	162	251	337	494	337
HMG	166	108	108	112	111	166
AA MG	33	27	12	9	0	18
AT Rifles	0	0	89	228	212	107
45mm AT Gun	54	18	30	30	48	54
37mm AA Gun	12	10	6	6	0	12
76mm Gun	34	28	28	32	32	44
122mm Howitzer	32	8	8	12	12	20
152mm Howitzer	12	0	0	0	0	0
Mortars	150	78	162	188	160	127

were fast becoming ineffective against the frontal armour of the Panzers. The Soviets failed to develop a rocket-propelled grenade, comparable to the German Panzerfaust or Panzerschreck, the American bazooka, or even a spigot projectile like the British PIAT. The Soviet infantry were forced to rely on anti-tank grenades or anti-tank mines. This is all the more surprising, as the Soviets were very active in the development of rocket artillery like the *Katyushas*, and had even worked on rocket anti-tank weapons before the war. However, the Red Army made extensive use of captured German Panzerfaust, and there is some evidence that the Soviets began manufacturing a copy in 1944–45 as the RPG-1. Soviet rifle regiments had a battery of 45mm anti-tank guns, and they became adept at using these for anti-tank defence.

The élite of the Red Army rifle forces during the war were the *razvedchiki*, the scouts. The Red Army did not form very many special purpose units, relying instead on scout units; usually, each rifle regiment would receive a company of scouts, and each division would have a battalion. Scouts were drawn from the best troops in the division, and were usually given preference in equipment, food and clothing. One of the more obvious signs of their élite distinction was the camouflage coverall worn by scout troops.

Red Army Cavalry

Sergeant Kalimulla Khabibulin, a Tatar tank commander, on his T-34 Model 1942 tank. His tank was credited with three German tanks and two self-propelled guns during fighting in 1942. He is wearing the winter issue black leather tankers' jacket and trousers. This was an expensive item, and so many tank crews were issued a *telogreika* instead, sometimes in tankers' black instead of the usual khaki.

The Red Army used cavalry forces more extensively than any other army during the Second World War. The Soviet cavalry forces had been substantially trimmed back after 1939, many of the old cavalry units forming the basis for new tank formations. The retention of this colourful and heroic branch was due to its prominent rôle in the 1917–21 Civil War, and to the personal sentiments of many of Stalin's old cavalry cronies like Budenny and Voroshilov. At the outset of the war there were nine cavalry divisions and four mountain cavalry divisions. They did not play a prominent rôle in the summer fighting; and in August 1941 their establishment was considerably reduced from a theoretical strength of 9,240 men to a new light cavalry division with only 3,000 men. Rather than disappearing, Soviet cavalry divisions expanded in number. By the end of 1941 they reached 82 divisions. However, it should be noted that these formations were so small that they were really equivalent to brigades. They were normally formed into corps with two or three divisions, these cavalry corps being closer to a true division in strength.

The sudden expansion of the cavalry was due to the severe weakness of the Red Army in modern mechanised forces. The cavalry branch was used primarily as mounted infantry, and for scouting. In the wild Russian terrain, and in bad weather conditions, cavalry were usually more mobile than motorised formations on trucks. Indeed, the Soviets successfully used cavalry units alongside tank units in curious mobile attack groups. Even the Germans realized the utility of cavalry under the conditions of the Eastern Front, and expanded their mounted forces after their experiences in the winter of 1941–42. The year 1942 was the heyday of the Red Army cavalry. In part this was because Russian cavalry had traditionally come from the southern lands, where much of the 1942 fighting took place. As mentioned above, many national cavalry divisions were formed from Central Asian troops. The decline of Soviet cavalry was due to the revitalisation in the summer of 1942 of the Soviet mechanised formations which took over the burden of mobile operations. By the summer of 1943 the cavalry had been trimmed back to 27 divisions. Cavalry continued to serve right through to the end of the war, however. During Operation 'Bagration' in Byelorussia in the summer of 1944, the 3rd

A Soviet *razvedchik* scout consults with partisans in a mountain pass in the Caucasus during the fighting there in 1942. The Red Army actively sponsored an extensive partisan force behind German lines throughout the war, and often used the *razvedchiki* as couriers between regular army and irregular partisan forces. The scout is wearing the two-piece camouflage coveralls, and a Tokarev TT pistol holster on an officer's leather belt.

Guards Mechanised Corps was linked up with the 3rd Guards Cavalry Corps to form a special Horse-Mechanised Group (KMG) which was used with considerable success in the wooded areas of the western USSR. One of the most famous cavalry operations of the war came in August 1945, with the attacks of the KMG under Gen.Col. I. A. Pliyev in the short war with Japan in Manchuria.

Tank and Mechanised Forces

Although the tank and mechanised forces of the Red Army amounted to only a tenth of the army's strength, they had a disproportionate influence on its eventual victory. The mechanised forces in 1941 were massive: numbering 29 mechanised corps, each with two tank and one motor rifle divisions, they were far larger than the Panzer units of the invading Wehrmacht. Indeed, the Germans had only about 3,500 tanks against about 28,000 Soviet armoured vehicles. But the Soviet mechanised force of 1941 was a paper tiger; by December 1941, the

Soviets had only about 2,000 tanks left to confront the Germans in European Russia.

The Soviet tank force in 1941 was made up primarily of T-26 infantry tanks and BT cavalry tanks. These tanks have often been excessively disparaged; in fact, they were capable designs, a bit light on armour, but well armed with a 45mm gun. They were certainly comparable to the German PzKpfw II, which still made up a significant part of the Panzer force. Their main problem lay not in their design, but in their state of repair. The massive build-up of the Red Army in the 1930s reflected an obsession with numbers. Soviet factories churned out large quantities of tanks and armoured cars; but many were defective, and the factories largely ignored the mundane question of spare parts. As a result, by 1941 44 per cent were broken down and in need of rebuilding, and 26 per cent needed significant repair. Soviet tank units left a stream of broken-down tanks behind them as they retreated.

The Soviet tank force was in the process of rebuilding with a new generation of excellent new designs, including the T-34 medium tank and the

KV heavy tank.[1] The T-34 was a revolutionary design and a major advance in tank technology. The T-34 and KV gave the Germans a real shock in 1941; however, they had no decisive impact on the fighting, for two reasons. To begin with, both vehicles were very new and suffered from serious technical problems. They had been rushed into production, and suffered from mechanical problems with their engines and transmissions which led to excessive breakdowns. Secondly, Soviet mechanised tactics were equally immature, especially when facing an experienced tank force like the German Panzerwaffe.

In the late summer of 1941 the Red Army abandoned all large armoured formations, abolishing the mechanised corps and disbanding most of the surviving tank divisions. The Soviet comman-

[1]See Vanguard 14, *The T-34 Tank*, and Vanguard 24, *Soviet Heavy Tanks*.

15

Although there were specific clothing items for women in the Red Army, those assigned to the front lines usually wore the same field dress as men. Senior Lieutenant Alexandra Tsvetkova is wearing the normal winter-issue *gymnastiorka* and trousers, and carries the standard medic's musette bag. Her one concession to official women's dress regulations is the pre-war dark blue beret.

they were divisions. The first use of the new formations in the summer of 1942 was very discouraging, and several of the new units were virtually wiped out by the veteran German Panzer force. But the Soviets gained experience in handling these new units, and by the winter of 1942 the tank and mechanised corps were finally replacing the cavalry as the Red Army's fast, mobile force. The record of tank and mechanised corps in the savage winter fighting around Stalingrad in January 1943 showed that the Soviet tank force had finally come of age.

The T-34 had finally had the bugs wrung out of it, and was proving a very capable design. The KV tank, in many respects, was a disappointment; though it was very well armoured, its gun was the same as that used on the T-34, but its mobility was not as good. Soviet tank battalions at the beginning of 1942 were mixed, fielding a company of KVs, a company of T-34s and a company of light tanks. This mixture proved impractical, and as the year dragged on the Soviets gradually developed homogenous tank brigades based around the T-34 alone. KV heavy tanks were relegated to independent tank regiments for infantry support, as their slow speed made them unsuitable for use in T-34 formations.

Soviet tactical shortcomings stemmed from two main areas of difficulty: training and vehicle design. Soviet tank training, like most Soviet training during the war, was constrained by the enormous demand for manpower. The average Red Army tanker received considerably less training than his German counterpart. For example, German tankers were very critical of Soviet driver training. Soviet tanks often drove along the crest of hills or along predictable routes since this made driving easier; they did not make use of terrain to hide their vehicles from enemy fire.

Also important were deficiencies in Soviet tank design. Soviet tanks during the war focused on the big three: armour, mobility and firepower. Soviet tanks were usually on an equal footing with German tanks when judged by these criteria. Their main shortcomings were in crew management. In

ders did not have the experience, skill or equipment to handle these enormous units. Instead, they went back to basics. The new formations were tank brigades, roughly equivalent to a (Western) battalion of tanks with a motor rifle company added to round it off. By the summer of 1942 the Soviets had gained enough confidence in the use of armour that they began forming larger armoured units again. The new tank and mechanised corps were corps in name only; by Western standards,

A Soviet *razvedchik* scout in the northern Caucasus, October 1942. He is armed with a captured German MP38 and wears the usual two-piece camouflage coverall favoured by the scouts.

The archetypal Soviet riflemen in action, Stalingrad, November 1942. This is standard dress: the Model 1940 helmet, rolled greatcoat, high boots and PPSh sub-machine gun. These riflemen also have entrenching tools, a rare item.

the early years of the war the T-34 and KV used an archaic crew configuration with the commander doubling as loader. This distracted him from his main tasks of locating targets and directing the tank. German tanks used three-man turret crews, leaving the commander free to command. The Soviet tanks also suffered from extremely poor commander's stations. German tank commanders generally operated with their head outside, scanning the horizon. Soviet tanks were poorly suited to this, and on early versions of the T-34 and KV it was virtually impossible for the commander to operate in this fashion. That the Soviets appreciated these deficiencies is evident in the tanks that began to appear in 1943 like the T-34/85, and IS-2. However, the Soviets continued to build the

wretched little T-60 and T-70 into 1943, largely because the automobile plants that manufacture them were incapable of building the larger T-34. I 1943 they switched to the SU-76 assault gun, whic became a staple of the infantry formations.

The summer campaign of 1943 saw the large armoured confrontation of the war in the are around Kursk-Orel. On a tactical level, Soviet tan units still had many lessons to learn from th Germans; but on an operational level the Sovi commanders were very adept in the use of mobil forces, and the Germans finally lost strateg initiative on the Eastern Front. By 1943 the quali gap between the Soviet and German tank crew narrowed greatly. German training began to sl down to the Soviet level.

The German adoption of the Panther as the new main battle tanks in 1943 forced the Soviets switch the balance of their tank programmes i 1944–45. The Soviets had become very dissatisfie with heavy tanks due to problems with the KV, and had allowed heavy tanks to fade away by the summer of 1943; but with the appearance of the Panther, they were forced to reinvigorate their heavy tank units. They responded with the IS-2 Stalin. Although called a 'heavy' tank by the Soviets, it was in fact in the same size and weight class as the Panther. After 1943 the new, upgunned T-34/85 made up the bulk of the Soviet tank force, but heavy armour like the IS-2 (and its tank destroyer cousins the ISU-122 and ISU-152) made up a larger percentage of the Red Army mechanised force than ever before.

Other Combat Branches

The Air Assault Force

The Red Army was the first European army to experiment with airborne forces on a large scale. Soviet paratroopers were used in the war with Finland, and during the occupation of Romanian Bessarabia in 1940. At the outset of the war in 1941 there were five airborne VDV (Airborne Assault Force) corps in Europe and a brigade in the Far East. Soviet airborne operations during the Second World War were hampered by the lack of transport aircraft. The Luftwaffe shot up most of the TB-3 heavy transport aircraft in June 1941, and the VDV units had to make do with transports obtained from the civilian Aeroflot. As a result, the airborne corps were used mainly as élite infantry during the 1941 fighting.

The first major airborne operations of the war began in January 1942, but a combination of weather and lack of airlift doomed them to failure. The largest of these operations was an attempt to drop the 4th Airborne Corps into the Vyazma area: it was a fiasco. To airlift the corps in a single jump would have required 600 aircraft; they had 22. The air drops began on 27 January and were not completed until 23 February, in very rough winter

In 1942–43 the Red Army raised a number of national cavalry divisions in Central Asia, this squadron in Kirghizia. Several of the cavalrymen wear the Kirghiz fur cap, while others wear a *kubanka* or Red Army *ushanka*. The unit is obviously of mixed composition, including both Kirghiz and European Soviets.

Nikolai P. Galchenko fought as a partisan in the Sumy area of the Ukraine, joining up with the Red Army in 1943, and serving in a machine gun unit of the 615th Rifle Regt., 167th Rifle Division. During the fighting for Kiev he overcame a number of German positions, earning the highest Soviet military distinction, the Hero of the Soviet Union award. He died of wounds received in December 1943. He is wearing winter snow coveralls; some of these were cut greatcoat-fashion, as here, while others were of a more conventional coveralls cut with legged trousers.

conditions. The Corps was badly scattered, and ended up fighting its way back to Soviet lines in isolated groups until June 1942. As a result of the lack of aircraft in 1942, the remaining airborne corps were first converted to Guards Rifle Divisions, only to be reconverted back to Guards Airborne Divisions beginning in September 1942. Most remained in service as infantry units in spite of their titles. The last major airborne drop in the European theatre took place in September 1943 when the 1st, 3rd and 5th Guards Airborne Brigades were dropped over the Dnepr River to secure a bridgehead. It was a bloody failure. The Soviets conducted a number of small-scale drops using naval infantry and improvised army units,

but in general Soviet operations in the Great Patriotic War were failures.[1]

The Artillery

Soviet artillery was the killing arm of the Red Army in the Second World War. Soviet sources claim that it accounted for 60–80 per cent of enemy casualties. Although the artillery was very important in the fighting, it lost the decisive impact it had possessed in the First World War, largely due to the decisive contribution of armoured vehicles and the more mobile nature of the war. Soviet artillery had long been the favourite combat branch of the Russian Army; it attracted many of the most skilled weapons designers and talented officers.

At the outset of the war, rifle divisions were equipped with two artillery regiments with 76mm, 122mm and 152mm guns and howitzers. The heavy losses of equipment in 1941 led to major cuts in divisional artillery; this was reduced to one regiment with a battalion of 76mm guns (like the ZIS-3) and another with 122mm howitzers. In addition, each rifle regiment had a battery of short-barrelled 76mm regimental guns. Guns above 122mm howitzers were retained in Front and Army level units. Rifle divisions came to depend very heavily on mortars to supplement their tubed artillery. Divisional artillery expanded later in the war, mostly in terms of quantity of tubes.

The Soviets tended to concentrate their growing artillery force, such as the High Command Reserve (VGK Reserve). At the outset of the war this force amounted to only about 8 per cent of the artillery but by the war's end it amounted to 35 per cent. The new VGK Reserve included artillery divisions, and in 1943, special artillery breakthrough corps. The VGK Reserve also controlled smaller regiments equipped with special large calibre weapons. These units were centrally controlled and allotted to Armies and Fronts depending on the importance of their missions.

The Soviets favoured the multiple rocket launchers—the legendary Katyusha—to a greater extent than most other armies. Katyushas were well suited to the Russian predilection for massed firepower. They could deliver a very heavy concentration of fire in a very short space of time

[1] For further details on the history of the VDV, see Elite 5, *Soviet Bloc Elite Forces.*

A *razvedchiki* detachment on patrol. Both scouts are armed with the PPSh sub-machine gun, and the soldier to the right holds an RG-42 hand grenade.

operation, it was often up to 375 guns and mortars on a kilometre of front—a truly earth-shaking barrage.

The Soviets never developed a mechanised artillery force during the war, favouring conventional towed artillery. Self-propelled guns like the SU-85 and SU-100 were designed as tank destroyers. Heavy assault guns like the ISU-122 and ISU-152 were direct-fire weapons, usually manned by tank troops, and not intended for the artillery's traditional indirect fire rôle. The ubiquitous SU-76 assault gun was used mainly for direct fire support of the infantry, though it was capable of being used for indirect fire.

compared to conventional tubed artillery. Their elementary construction also appealed to the Soviets. Conventional artillery requires elaborate machine tools to manufacture and rifle the barrel; Katyusha launchers use simple rails that can be built by a small machine shop. The Katyushas were officially called 'Guards Mortars' in the Red Army during the war; by the war's end, there were seven Guards Mortar divisions compared with 30 regular artillery divisions.

German artillery officers were impressed by the volume of Soviet artillery fire, but not by the conduct of fire. They felt that Soviet artillery was too predictable, and too often favoured area bombardment over precisely targeted strikes. The Germans also found that in the first years of the war the Soviets largely concentrated on targets along the immediate front, often ignoring targets in the deep rear. However, the Germans conceded that Soviet tactics improved greatly as the war went on. If the German artillery officers were sometimes contemptuous of their opponents, the same was not true for the German infantry. To front-line troops, Soviet artillery was a much feared and respected arm. The situation grew worse in the later years of the war as Soviet artillery increased in volume. During operations in 1941–42 Soviet artillery strength was seldom higher than 70–80 guns and mortars per kilometre in a major attack sector. By the summer of 1944 it had risen to 220 guns and mortars per kilometre of front where a major attack was taking place. By the time of the Berlin

Naval Infantry

The Soviet Navy, especially the surface fleet, saw very little action after the initial fighting in the summer of 1941. The Baltic Fleet was largely bottled up in Leningrad. The Black Sea Fleet, although more active, was often bottled up in port by German air power. As a result, the Navy became a reserve of idle personnel. The Navy traditionally had naval infantry brigades attached to the fleets which could be committed to land combat. In October 1941, 25 new naval infantry brigades were formed, which fought alongside Red Army formations, and ten more were added later. They were most heavily committed on the Leningrad Front, but also took part in the defence of Moscow, and were very active in the fighting in 1942 along the Black Sea. Besides these regular formations, many fleets formed improvised battalions and small units during the course of the war. Naval infantry took part in over a hundred small-scale amphibious landings, mainly in the Black Sea area.

NKVD Security Forces

Aside from combat units of the Red Army, Soviet state security forces fielded a large number of combat units during the war. In 1941 the NKVD was responsible for the Border Troops who patrolled along the frontier, and these took a very active part in the initial fighting of June 1941. The war also saw a major expansion in the NKVD Internal Troops. These units were organised like rifle or cavalry divisions and were intended to maintain internal order in the Soviet Union. At the beginning of the war the NKVD formed 15 rifle

The 16th Lithuanian Infantry Division was one of a number of 'national' divisions formed during the war. Although the uniform of the unit was mostly standard Red Army issue, some small national details were permitted, such as the arm-of-service lozenge on the upper arm displayed by this infantry junior lieutenant (foreground) and artillery officer.

Red Army Uniforms

At the outset of the war in 1941, Red Army uniforms were based on *Prikaz 176*, the 3 December 1935 dress regulations. For generals, there were three basic categories of uniforms: everyday, walking-out and parade. For officers and enlisted men, the three categories were everyday, guard (*karaulniy*) and walking-out. In the case of all three categories, there was both a summer and a winter version. Although not noted in the official categories, in practice there was usually detail differences between the uniforms and insignia worn by senior officers and junior officers. Between 1935 and 1941 there were numerous small changes to the uniforms, especially to those worn by generals. The focus of this description is on field uniforms, and most of these dress uniforms will be ignored.

The 1940 Rank Insignia

During the Bolshevik Revolution and subsequent Civil War, traditional ranks were abolished, as well as the traditional shoulderboard. As the years passed this political decision was increasingly seen to be preposterous, and the Red Army gradually reintroduced rank. The new insignia intentionally avoided traditional Russian insignia and ranks, although national elements continued to creep back in throughout the early 1940s. In July 1940 the rank insignia introduced in 1936 were modified. It was the 1940 pattern insignia sequence which the Red Army used in the first years of the war.

There were three basic elements to rank and service insignia. The insignia was worn on the collar in one of two forms: a rectangular tab for most uniforms, and a patch for the greatcoat. There were four basic categories of officers: marshals and generals, who wore embroidered stars; senior officers (*komdiv*, *kombrig*) with red enamelled diamonds with gold trim; middle commanders (colonels to captains), with enamelled rectangles; and junior officers (lieutenants) with enamelled squares. Junior leaders (sergeants) wore enamelled triangles. Officers' insignia was also worn in the form of an embroidered chevron worn on the forearm. (The sleeve insignia was abandoned early in the war as ordered by *Prikaz 253* on 1 August 1941.)

divisions. At times of crisis, these units were committed to the front like regular rifle divisions. Indeed, the NKVD formed some of them into Special Purpose (*Spetsnaz*) Armies, and one of these was used during the breakthroughs in the Crimea. However, this was not their primary rôle. They were intended to stiffen the resistance of the Red Army, and during major operations were often formed into 'blocking detachments' which collected stragglers and prevented retreats. Their other rôle was to hunt out anti-Soviet partisan groups, and to carry out punitive expeditions against ethnic groups suspected of collaborating with the Germans.

The NKVD special troops were expanded in the final years of the war, eventually totalling 53 divisions and 28 brigades, not counting the Border Troops. This was equal to about a tenth of the total number of regular Red Army rifle divisions. These units were used in the prolonged partisan wars in the Ukraine and the Baltic republics which lasted until the early 1950s. They were also involved in the wholesale deportations of suspected ethnic groups in 1943–45. In some respects, the NKVD formations resembled the German Waffen-SS in terms of independence from the normal military structure. However, the NKVD troops were used mainly for internal security and repression, and were not heavily enough armed for front-line combat. Unlike the Waffen-SS, they had no major armoured or mechanised formations.

Rank	Tab Insignia
Marshal	Star, wreath
Army General	5 stars
General Colonel	4 stars
General Lieutenant	3 stars
General Major	2 stars
Komkor	3 diamonds
Komdiv	2 diamonds
Kombrig	1 diamond
Colonel	4 rectangles
Lt. Colonel	3 rectangles
Major	2 rectangles
Captain	1 rectangle
Sr.Lieutenant	3 squares
Lieutenant	2 squares
Jr.Lieutenant	1 square
Sergeant Major	4 triangles
Sr.Sergeant	3 triangles
Sergeant	2 triangles
Jr.Sergeant	1 triangle

Service colours

The branch of service was indicated by coloured piping and by service insignia. The background colour of the tab indicated the service, and was complemented by a small gold branch insignia on the tab. For officers, the tab was trimmed in gold embroidery or metal; for enlisted men, the piping was in the service colour. For sergeants, the tab was trimmed in the service colour, but a narrow red band ran across the tab to distinguish it from the enlisted men. The peaked cap of officers had a band in the service colour; for enlisted men, the *pilotka* side cap carried piping in the service colours. Uniform piping was also in service colours. It

Red Army Rank Insignia: April 1941 Subdued Pattern. *A*: General of the Army; *B*: General Colonel; *C*: General Lieutenant; *D*: General Major; *E*: Corps Commander; *F*: Division Commander; *G*: Brigade Commander; *H*: Colonel; *I*: Lieutenant-Colonel; *J*: Major; *K*: Captain; *L*: Senior Lieutenant; *M*: Lieutenant; *N*: Junior Lieutenant; *O*: Sergeant Major; *P*: Senior Sergeant; *Q*: Sergeant; *R*: Junior Sergeant; *S*: Private. (Greatcoat collar tab above, *gymnastiorka* collar tab below.)

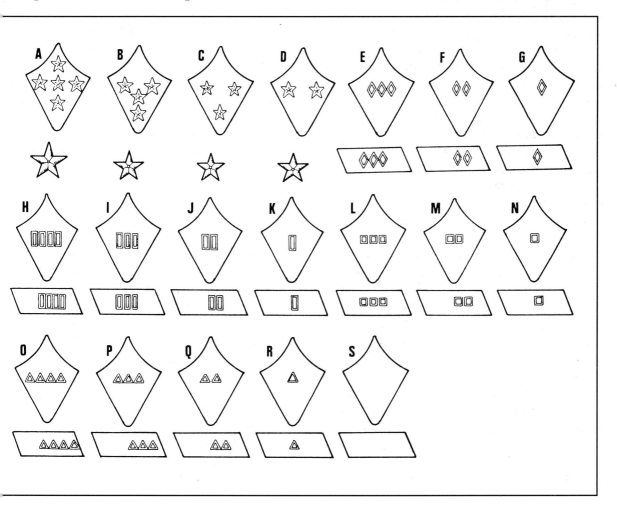

should be noted that the various branches did not have a single colour: rather, there was a pattern of colours for each branch, which are summarised in the table on page 33.

A unique position in the Army was the political officer, or *kommisar*. Kommisars were usually assigned to units of battalion size and greater. At the time of the purges in 1937 a junior political officer, or *politruk*, was added for lower formations. Kommisars generally wore the same insignia as officers of the service in which they served, with some small differences. They wore a star insignia instead of a chevron on the sleeve; kommisars had black trim on the collar tabs rather than officers' gold, but politruks had piping in the same colour as the unit they served in.

In January 1941 the Red Army began to take steps to modify their uniforms to make them more suitable for wartime conditions. This mainly affected the colourful collar tabs and other insignia, and new variants began to be manufactured in subdued colours. The tab itself was manufactured

Soviet Rank Insignia: Shoulder boards 1943. *A*: **Marshal of the Soviet Union;** *B*: **Chief Marshal (Artillery);** *C*: **Marshal (Armoured Force);** *D*: **General of the Army;** *E*: **General Colonel;** *F*: **General Lieutenant;** *G*: **General Major;** *H*: **Colonel (Rifle Forces);** *I*: **Lieutenant-Colonel (Artillery);** *J*: **Major (Armoured Force);** *K*: **Captain (Cavalry);** *L*: **Senior Lieutenant (Railway Troops);** *M*: **Lieutenant (Sappers);** *N*: **Junior Lieutenant (Bridging Troops);** *O*: **Sergeant Major;** *P*: **Senior Sergeant;** *Q*: **Sergeant;** *R*: **Junior Sergeant;** *S*: **Corporal;** *T*: **Private.**

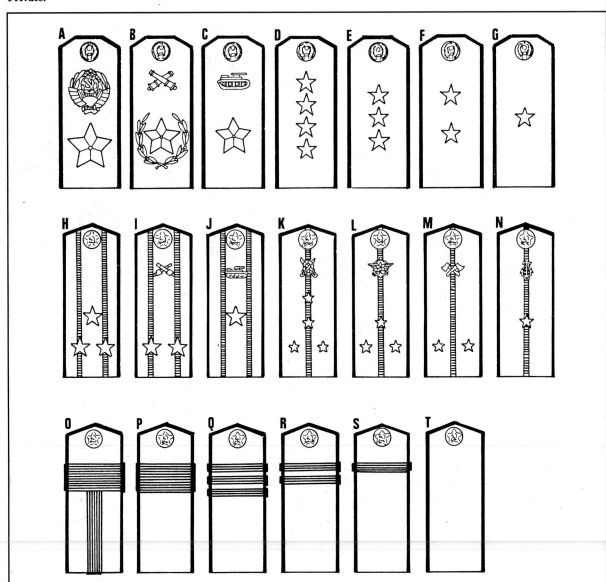

The Defence of the Brest Fortress, 1941:
1: Lieutenant, NKVD Border Troops
2: Senior Battalion Kommisar, Red Army
3: Red Army rifleman

A

The Defence of Leningrad, 1941-42:
1: Sergeant, Red Army Rifle Forces
2: Lieutenant, Red Army Medical Branch
3: Naval Infantryman, Baltic Fleet

B

The Defence of Moscow, 1941-42:
1: Sergeant-Major, Red Army Rifle Forces
2: Red Army rifleman
3: Tank crewman, 1st Moscow Mot. Rifle Div.

C

The Battle for Stalingrad, 1942-43:
1: Red Army, anti-tank rifleman
2: Red Army rifleman
3: Senior sergeant, Red Army Tank Forces

Red Army Cossack Cavalry:
1: Captain, Kuban Cossacks
2: Officer, Kuban Cossacks, winter dress
3: Lieutenant, Terek Cossacks, field dress

E

The Battle of Kursk, 1943:
1: Red Army tank crewman
2: Red Army sniper
3: Lieutenant, Red Army Rifle Forces

F

Operation 'Bagration', 1944:
1: Red Army scout
2: Sergeant, Red Army Traffic Control
3: Red Army sniper

G

The Battle for Berlin, 1945:
1: Red Army anti-tank grenadier
2: Junior Lt., Red Army Artillery
3: NKVD Internal Security Officer

H

in a drab green/khaki without the usual service colour piping, and the enamelled insignia gave way to plain metal insignia. The small service insignia were usually removed from the tabs. The plan was to introduce these changes from October 1941 through 1942, but the plan was interrupted by hostilities. However, it became increasingly uncommon to see the peacetime rank insignia after the first few months of the war.

Field Dress and Equipment

Soviet Model 1935 field uniforms were in varying shades of khaki drab, called *zashchitniy tsvet* in Russian. The most distinctive element of the field uniform was the *gymnastiorka*, a simple blouse resembling the traditional peasant shirt. The cut of both the officers' and enlisted ranks' gymnastiorka was similar. The breast pocket flaps of the officers' blouse dipped into a 'V' below the button-hole, while on the enlisted ranks' blouse, the pocket often had a straight cut. The fly flap covering the front buttons on the officers' blouse terminated in an inverted triangle, while on the enlisted ranks' blouse, the reinforcing patch was square. The rankers' blouse also had a reinforcing patch running under the forearm and flaring at the elbow, or with a diamond reinforcing patch at the elbow. The peacetime version of the officers' gymnastiorka had coloured piping at the wrist which was absent on the rankers' blouse; this was dropped by the 1941 order.

There were two issues of gymnastiorka, summer weight and winter weight. The summer blouse was made of cotton, and often faded to a lighter khaki shade; the winter issue was wool, and usually remained a more olive-green shade of khaki. Officers wore the gymnastiorka with a Sam Browne belt with a brass buckle embossed with a Soviet star. The enlisted men wore a simple leather belt with an ordinary open buckle. There were two other types of tunic-shirts that could be seen in the field. Although intended for walking-out wear, the officers had a khaki tunic called a 'French' which was sometimes seen in action. (This was named after the British general, not the country.) Some enlisted men could be seen with a special gymnastiorka with a coloured band running down the button flap; this was a special issue item to élite rifleman units, and was not common.

Both officers and enlisted men were issued a traditional Russian *sharovari*, a type of 'semi-breeches' trousers which flare at the hip like riding breeches. The enlisted men's version had a diamond-shape reinforcing patch at the knee. Officers were issued with black leather boots, while enlisted men either had the old pattern low boots with puttees, or a cheaper, leather or tarpaulin *sapogi* high boot. For winter wear, both officers and men were issued with a brownish-grey greatcoat, the officers' coat differing in details and quality. Headgear was diverse. Most units retained the *shelm*, a cloth peaked cap more popularly called the *budionovka* after the dashing Civil War cavalry officer, Semyon Budenny. This came in both summer- and winter-weight versions. The summer weight version was gradually replaced by the *pilotka* side cap for enlisted men during the late 1930s. Officers generally wore a peaked cap with summer dress, and the shelm for winter dress. In Central Asia, the Far East, and in certain élite units, a

Branch Colours, 1940

Service	Collar Tab	Tab Piping*	Uniform Piping	Cap Band or Piping
Infantry	raspberry	black	raspberry	raspberry
Cavalry	blue	black	lt. blue	black
Artillery	black	red	red	red
Technical forces	black**	blue	black**	black**
Chemical forces	black**	black	black**	black**
Services	dk. green**	red	red	red

*Gold trim for officers   **Raspberry for generals

One of the earliest combat postings for Russian women was sniper duty. Snipers were volunteers, often with pre-war sporting backgrounds. These two snipers, R. Skrypnikova and O. Bykova, return from a mission in September 1943, wearing the two-piece camouflage coveralls issued to scouts and snipers.

which was made of brown leather, but this was very uncommon after 1941. A modern field pack, the Model 1938, was also in use. It was in khaki-green fabric with leather trim, with two outside pockets, and was about 12 in. square and 4 in. deep (30 × 10cm). The inside section carried underwear, *portyanki*, and cape/shelter half, and the outside pockets contained rifle accessories and toilet items. Underneath the pack there were straps to attach tent-poles, pegs and other tent gear. There were also loops on the top and sides to attach the greatcoat in horseshoe fashion. A ration pouch was worn attached to the belt underneath the field pack, in the small of the back. A lined fabric pouch about 7 in. deep, 9 in. wide and 4 in. thick (18 × 24 × 10cm), it contained dry rations, the mess kit and spoon-fork. The standard mess kit was an aluminium container, resembling the German type, with a tight-fitting cover and clamp handle. Some units also used the older circular pattern pot which was 6 in. in diameter and about 4 in. deep (15 × 10cm). Both the Model 1938 field pack and ration pouch were expensive to manufacture and became uncommon after 1941.

Troops were issued with gasmasks and gasmask musette bags. After the outbreak of war many of the masks were thrown away and the bags used to carry rations, ammunition and other kit due to the lack of the Model 1938 field pack and ration bag. Officially, riflemen received two standard Moisin-Nagant leather rifle cartridge pouches, each taking four clips for a total of 20 rounds. They were

broad-brimmed 'panama' cotton sun hat replaced the pilotka in 1938.

In 1936, the Soviets introduced a new steel helmet to replace a Russian adaptation of the French Adrian helmet. This 1936 helmet was still in widespread service in 1941, even though yet another improved helmet was introduced in 1940. Memoirs of Soviet officers recall the difficulties they had in convincing men to wear helmets: many Russian soldiers found them uncomfortable, and regarded wearing them as 'sissy' and unmanly. Officers generally wore the peaked cap, even in units with steel helmets, as a method of distinguishing rank. Armoured troops had a special reinforced helmet made of leather or duck, available in both summer and fur-lined winter weights.

Soviet equipment was austere and elementary. Some units still had the old Model 1930 rucksack,

Guards Sergeants Mikhail Fironov and Mikhail Vasiliev of a *razvedchiki* scout detachment tuning an RBM-1 man-portable radio. Scout units often used radios in the later years of the war when on deep reconnaissance missions.

supposed to be worn on the belt, one to either side. In addition, a fabric reserve ammunition pouch was issued carrying a further six clips, or 30 rounds of rifle ammunition. A fabric ammunition bandoleer was also available, slung diagonally over the shoulder, carrying 14 five-round clips. A grenade pouch was also developed, carrying two-stick grenades. This was about 9 × 5 in. (23 × 13cm) and had a flap cover. Very few troops were actually issued this extensive selection of field equipment. Indeed, most simply had a single leather Moisin-Nagant ammunition pouch, usually worn on the right side of the belt. Many troops were issued with an entrenching shovel and fabric cutter, worn over the right hip. The canteen, when available, was usually attached to the belt over this.

For poor weather troops were issued with a cape/shelter half, called a *plashch-palatka*. This was made of a dark olive fabric, and had a drawstring hood. Two of these could be combined to form a small two-man tent, or a larger four- or six-man tent could be formed with additional capes. When wearing the Model 1938 field pack, the cape/shelter half, with the greatcoat inside, was carried horseshoe style around the pack. When not wearing the pack, the shelter or greatcoat was made into a bedroll and worn diagonally over the chest in the traditional fashion.

Officers had a small musette bag of either leather or fabric. There were different patterns, some on a strap worn over the shoulders, others attached to the belt; worn in lieu of a field pack, this musette included a small map case. Other officers wore a larger, leather dispatch/map case, usually attached to the belt, under the left arm.

There were a variety of specialised uniforms. Tankers were issued black coveralls, and had black leather jackets (and sometimes trousers) for winter wear. Mountain troops had a special black two-piece coverall as well as specialised climbing shoes. The cavalry, especially the Cossack units, wore traditional ethnic garb, which is covered in the Plates commentaries.

The German invasion of 1941 had a devastating effect on Soviet war industries; the Germans managed to capture most of the major industrial cities by the end of 1941. The Soviets saved large numbers of the machine tools, however, which were sent east to new factories in the Urals. The

Men of a Don Cossack cavalry division attached to the Second Ukrainian Front rest in woods in the western Ukraine, May 1944. In the foreground, a corporal sharpens his sabre with a whetstone. He wears the pre-war blue trousers with a red stripe. Above the Guards insignia on his right breast are two wound stripes: a gold stripe indicated a heavy wound, a red stripe a light wound. Behind him a woman medic tends the wounds of a lieutenant; from her shoulderboards, the medic is a sergeant major. The lieutenant wears the *kubanka* fur cap, popular in Cossack cavalry regiments.

industrial losses forced the Soviets to adopt austerity measures which were most severely felt in 1942. The winter fighting of 1941–42 forced the introduction of more suitable winter gear. This was covered in the August 1941 decree, but Soviet equipment became very austere compared to the 1941 pattern. The new winter gear had been under development since the embarrassing Finnish campaign of 1939–40. It included the *telogreika* padded jacket, the *vatnie sharovari* padded trousers and the *shapka-ushanka* synthetic fur cap. Officers were entitled to a new sheepskin jacket, the *polushubok*, if available; in many cases, a full-length sheepskin coat, the *shuba*, was substituted in its

A scout patrol crawls forward. These scouts have the less common *mochalniy* style of camouflage coveralls with the simulated foliage made of tassels of fabric.

for extremely cold temperatures. Some units did requisition civilian supplies of these boots, but most units had to rely on old army *kirozoviy sapogi*, a high boot using an impregnated tarpaulin fabric in lieu of leather. The only advantage of these boots was that they were so loose that they could be stuffed with newspaper or cloth for added insulation. Soviet soldiers were not issued socks; instead, they received the traditional *portyanki*, narrow strips of linen or cotton which were wrapped around the foot. Normal socks were impractical with the loose boots, and were too much of a luxury for the common soldier; however, officers were issued socks, when available. Some units did receive a special type of *valenki*, much prized, that had a special rubberised coating on the lower portion, which made them especially suitable in the autumn rains and spring thaw when mud and slush could be atrocious.

In 1942 Soviet uniforms were characterised by a distinct lack of 'uniformity'. Textile factories turned out the best they could. Tankers' coveralls, which were supposed to be black, could be seen in dark blue, dark grey, and even khaki. Synthetic materials began to be developed to fill in for scarce materials such as leather and rubber. Cartridge pouches were made of fabric, or of an impregnated fabric designed to look like leather. Leather belts gave way to canvas.

Blankets were not issued to Soviet troops, who were expected to make do with the greatcoat or shelter cape. The greatcoat or shelter cape was also used to make a simple bed-roll to carry personal items when rucksacks were not available. A simple rucksack was developed, patterned on the old Tsarist Model 1915 style, called the *veshchevoi meshok*. It was really nothing more than a sack with a drawstring at the top, with a pair of canvas straps sewn on. Further diversity was introduced as Lend-Lease clothing began to arrive, mainly from the USA and Canada. Although much of the clothing was manufactured to Soviet design, there was a significant amount of American and Canadian pattern material supplied as well. For example, the USA supplied 13 million pairs of leather shoes, and one million pairs of soldiers' low boots, and Canada produced Soviet tankers' coveralls.

The various uniform decrees also set out specialised clothing for women in the army. Before

place. Senior officers (over colonel) were issued the *papakha* high fur cap instead of ushankas. In arctic areas, such as the front north of Leningrad, there were special provisions for winter field dress. In place of the sheepskin shuba, some units received the sealskin *sakui* coverall. These units also had a heavier grade of winter boot, usually with wool or dog-fur lining. The arctic ushanka was usually made of actual fur, either fox or dog.

Many units had no specialised winter wear, and many soldiers relied on the traditional greatcoat, supplemented by whatever civilian clothing could be acquired; indeed, one of the characteristic features of Soviet uniforms was the extent to which civilian clothing was adopted, especially during the winter months, due to a lack of army-issue winter equipment. For example, troops were supposed to be issued with *valenki*, a type of compressed felt boot,

the war this included a standard dark blue skirt, and a dark blue women's beret for walking-out and parade. Women's clothing was covered in uniform regulations in May and August of 1942. The beret and skirt were retained, in khaki for field dress and dark blue for parade. The orders brought women's clothing closer to the patterns of the 1941 orders for men. During the war it became increasingly difficult to manufacture specialised clothing for women troops, and many were simply issued standard men's uniforms. The women had to scavenge for themselves, and many were able to obtain, alter or make suitable clothing coinciding with the revised uniform orders. Many women soldiers wore parade uniform in certain staff and administrative rôles, while women in combat units or frontline service tended to wear the same clothing as male soldiers.

Camouflage Clothing

The experience in Finland led to the adoption of winter snow coveralls in 1941. These came in a variety of patterns, usually two-piece with a hood. The Soviets also introduced a two-piece camouflage suit for special forces, notably scouts, engineer scouts, mountain troops and snipers. Very

A medic tends a rifleman during the fighting against the Finns on the Karelian isthmus in the spring of 1944. The officer to the right is carrying a German stick grenade. The small-style canteen can be seen hanging from his Sam Browne belt, as well as the attachments for a map case. He is wearing a *telogreika* padded jacket with a rain cape rolled up in horseshoe fashion. The wounded soldier carries a map case as well, and is probably an officer, though the rain cape covers his shoulder boards.

baggy and loose-fitting, this was olive green with large rounded black splotches. Photos also show a special, reversible winter coverall that was green with white splotches on the inside; it is not clear when this was introduced, and it does not appear to have been very common. A special sniper coverall was developed, which had small tabs for attaching artificial string foliage, or actual foliage. It was made of a dark green fabric, and was relatively uncommon.

Cavalry Field Dress

The Red Army cavalry was certainly the most colourful branch, due to the retention of a variety of traditional Cossack dress. The majority of Soviet cavalry units were not Cossack formations, and their field dress was basically the same as ordinary Red Army field dress; however, many non-Cossack units took on elements of Cossack dress, especially

Austria, spring 1945. This is one of the least common styles of camouflage coveralls, with a light flecked pattern over dark green. The two soldiers to the rear wear the more common khaki/black style. This crew was issued the camouflage suits as they are part of an armoured scout unit; their vehicle is a Lend-Lease American M3A1 scout car.

the fur caps. During the war the Red Army recruited national Cossack cavalry divisions in the southern USSR, and largely left field dress up to the local units. The Soviets had mixed feelings about the Cossacks in the inter-war years due to the prominent rôle played by the Cossack cavalry on the side of anti-Bolshevik forces in the Civil War. However, in the 1930s Don, Kuban and Terek Cossack regiments did exist for a time, and the dress regulations did provide distinctive equipment. Field dress worn during the war was a combination of 1930s dress, pre-First World War dress, and 1940/1943 pattern field dress.

The Cossacks (Kazakh) are traditionally broken into two main groups: the Steppe Cossacks, like the Don Cossacks, and the Transcaucasian Cossacks, like the Terek and Kuban Cossacks. The style of field dress generally differed between these groups, with that of the Steppe Cossacks usually being less elaborate and closer to the rest of the army. The Cossacks generally wore a high wool cap, like the papashka, or a lower style adopted in the Red Army in the inter-war years, the *kubanka*. The Transcaucasian Cossacks could wear a dark blue or black shirt, called the *beshmet*; the dress version of this was red for the Kuban and light blue for the Terek Cossacks. This was covered by a dark blue or black kaftan called the *cherkeska*. The cherkeska was adorned with a diagonal pattern of decorative *gaziri* cartridge-tubes on either breast. In winter

they wore the traditional black shaggy wool cape, the *burka*. An item worn by many Cossacks was the *bashlyk*, a cape/scarf in different colours. The kubanka had a coloured cloth top, usually light blue for Terek and red for Kuban Cossacks, with gold braid (for officers) or black braid (for enlisted men) in a cross pattern over the centre. It should be noted that many Red Army soldiers in the southern USSR found these kubanka to be comfortable and attractive, and wore them instead of ushankas even though they were not in Cossack or even cavalry units. The Cossacks often wore dark blue breeches rather than the normal Red Army khaki.

The 1943 Uniform Changes

The most important changes in Soviet combat dress came in 1943. The Red Army significantly changed both its uniform and its insignia. The changes largely returned the Red Army to the Russian traditions of the First World War, Tsarist uniforms and insignia. The new orders temporarily abandoned the pre-war distinctions of everyday, walking-out and parade uniforms, which had become irrelevant under the war conditions, and basically covered field dress. Details of a form of parade dress were issued, primarily for troops on special guard duty, and for special occasions for officers. Walking-out dress was abandoned except for officers.

Prikaz 25 of 15 January 1943 laid down the new pattern gymnastiorka for both officers and enlisted men. This reverted to the Tsarist style, with a stand-up collar with two buttons. The enlisted men's gymnastiorka was without pockets while the officers' had two breast pockets. The trousers were unchanged from the previous pattern. The most noticeable change was the reversion to shoulder boards as a means of distinguishing rank. Two different styles were issued: everyday and field. The field shoulder boards were made in a basic khaki drab. The shoulder board was edged on three sides by piping in the service colour. On officers' shoulder boards, there were stripes running the length of the shoulder board; two for senior officers (major to colonel) and one for junior officers (junior lieutenant to captain). The stripes were in red except for medical, veterinary and non-combat branches, in which case they were in brown. Distinctions within these categories were displayed

Senior Lieutenant G. Iskaziev, a tank officer, credited with knocking out nine German tanks during one of the encirclement battles in the summer of 1941. This provides a good view of the pre-war pattern of collar tabs, as Iskaziev has pulled the collar of the greatcoat over the rain cape. The tab background is in the armoured branch colour, black, with the officers' trim of gold; the three squares are red enamel with a gold edge. The cap is made of grey wool, not khaki like other branches of the army, and has a black band with red piping. The collar tabs are visible under the greatcoat.

1943 Branch Colours

Branch	Colour	Emblem Colour
Infantry	Raspberry	(none)
Artillery	Red	Silver
Armour	Red	Silver
Cavalry	Blue	Silver
Technical	Black	Gold
Medical	Dk.green	Silver
NKVD	Blue	Silver or gold

Officers were issued with peaked service caps with a black patent leather brim. The cap had a coloured band with piping that varied by branch. Most caps were made of khaki cloth; however, armoured officers were supposed to have grey caps, NKVD Internal Security sky blue, and Don Cossacks blue-grey. The January 1943 decree also introduced a slightly modified winter headdress for officers: for colonels and above, the *papakha*, for other officers the standard ushanka.

1943 Officers' Service Caps

Branch	Band	Piping
Infantry	Raspberry	Raspberry
Artillery	Black	Red
Armour	Black	Red
Technical	Black	Blue
Cavalry	Blue	Black
Don Cossacks	Red	Red
Kuban/ Terek Cossacks	Blue	Red
NKVD	Red	Red

in the form of stars as listed below. The shoulder boards also carried a small silver or gold branch insignia, which was carried immediately outside the normal brass button. The colour of this emblem varied by branch, which is listed below along with the branch colours.

1943 Officers' Field Shoulder boards

Rank	Stars	Stripes
Colonel	3	2
Lt.Colonel	2	2
Major	1	2
Captain	4	1
Sr.Lieutenant	3	1
Lieutenant	2	1
Jr.Lieutenaant	1	1

Sergeants used a different system of rank stripes across the width of the shoulder board. These were in red, except for medical, veterinary and non-combat branches which were brown. Sergeant majors had a wide stripe with a lengthwise bar, giving the appearance of a 'T'. Senior sergeants had a single wide stripe, sergeants three narrow stripes, junior sergeants two stripes, and corporals one stripe. As in the case of officers' shoulder boards, the piping was in the branch colour. The branch insignia could be worn on the shoulder board, to the outside of the stripe; in practice it was not uncommon to see these metal insignia on the shoulder boards worn with field dress.

Although this book does not deal with Soviet naval uniforms, it is worth noting that in March

1944 a new decree was issued covering the naval infantry uniform with the aim of making it more practical for land warfare. Because the Soviet Navy was bottled up for most of the war, many sailors saw action as infantry, most notably in the siege of Leningrad and in the fighting in the Crimea. However, for most of the war they wore normal navy uniforms, with bits and pieces of army dress. The final uniform decree of the war was issued in April 1945 in anticipation of the victory. It provided generals with a new parade uniform, first seen at the 24 June 1945 victory parade in Moscow.

A Red Army rifle squad take cover during fighting for the port of Tolkemit in Germany, spring 1945. The squad is armed with a DT tank machine gun instead of the usual Degtaryev DP. The DT was popular with rifle units as it was smaller and lighter than the DP. The rifleman to the right wears a non-standard vest.

The Plates

A: The Defence of the Brest Fortress
A1: Lieutenant, NKVD Border Troops
This NKVD Border Troops lieutenant is in a mixture of walking-out dress and everyday wear. He is wearing the popular 'French' tunic, which was normally accompanied by dress trousers and walking shoes. However, he is wearing here the everyday *sharovari* pants, in dark blue with red piping, with high black boots. His field equipment includes the Sam Browne belt, Nagant pistol holster and map case. The basic service colour of the NKVD Border Troops was a bright medium green, evident on the peaked service cap and collar tabs, with the secondary dark blue colour evident on the cap band. The piping colour was red. The insignia for a lieutenant consisted of the two

The war's end: on the outskirts of Berlin, a Russian cavalryman talks with a Russian girl returning home after forced labour in Germany. He is wearing the standard rain cape over a *telogreika* jacket, and is armed with a Moisin Model 1938 carbine. In the background is an ISU-122 assault gun.

enamelled red squares on the collar tab, and the chevron on the sleeve in two alternating stripes of gold and red.

A2: Senior Battalion Kommisar, Red Army

This field dress consists of the 1936 pattern *gymnastiorka*, the normal *sharovari* trousers and high black leather boots. The collar tab, in medium blue with black piping, is that of the cavalry, as is the light blue piping on the uniform. Although officers in the line divisions were entitled to wear gold trim on the collar tabs, the political officers wore branch piping colours. The senior battalion kommisar wore three vertical rectangles, equivalent to a lieutenant colonel. The most distinctive element of the kommisar's insignia was the red worsted star with gold hammer and sickle, about 55mm in diameter and worn 80mm above the cuff. The cap is the same as that of a normal cavalry officer with a blue band and black piping. His field equipment consists of the brown leather Sam Browne belt, the dispatch case over the left hip and the Nagant pistol holster over the right.

A3: Red Army rifleman

This figure shows the complete regulation field equipment of a Red Army rifleman in 1941, although such a complete set is hardly typical. He is wearing the normal *gymnastiorka* with reinforced elbows, and the khaki *sharovari* pants with puttees and low black boots. At the centre of the equipment is the Model 1938 knapsack, which has the olive green *plashch-palatka* rain cape/shelter half wrapped around it. Underneath is attached the tent accessories pouch with stakes and tent poles. Below is the ration pouch. Over the right hip is the entrenching shovel in its khaki fabric carrier. Usually, the aluminium canteen was worn over this, in a khaki evaporation carrier. On his left hip is the grenade pouch for two stick grenades, and over and slightly in front of this is the BN gasmask musette bag. He is armed with the standard Moisin Model 1891 infantry rifle with the bayonet attached; with the exception of certain specialised

41

Guards Artillery Captain Stepan Chekurda, October 1942, in the full regalia of a Kuban Cossack. He is wearing the dark blue *cherkeska*, red shirt, and pre-war pattern collar tabs. His elegant *nagaika* dagger is carried on a decorated belt from which the *shashka* sabre is slung. He wears a black *papashka* fur cap with red star.

rifles like the Tokarev automatics, Soviet riflemen were not usually issued bayonet scabbards, since it was presumed that the bayonet would be left attached. He is wearing the Model 1940 steel helmet, painted in dark olive drab.

B: The Defence of Leningrad
B1: Sergeant, Red Army Rifle Forces
This sergeant is wearing the subdued patches introduced in the spring of 1941. The April 1941 changes removed the coloured elements of the insignia, replacing the collar tab backing with khaki. He is still wearing the old Model 1936 pattern helmet; often this helmet had a large red star painted on the front, as seen here. He is wearing normal field dress consisting of the Model 1936

enlisted men's *gymnastiorka*, the normal pants and black leather boots. He is carrying the old Tsarist pattern leather cartridge pouch, and is armed with a Moisin 1891/1907 carbine.

B2: Lieutenant, Red Army Medical Branch
This female medic is wearing the typical pre-war everyday wear consisting of a dark blue beret and skirt, and the Model 1936 *gymnastiorka* in the officers' pattern. She is carrying the standard issue medic's kit with a small red cross insignia. From her insignia, she is a lieutenant. Although medics could be armed, it was not the usual practice to issue women medics with weapons at this stage of the war.

B3: Baltic Fleet Naval Infantryman
At the outset of the war the Red Fleet did have naval infantry brigades; but the majority of Soviet seamen fighting ashore were normal sailors with no special infantry training, like this leading seaman of the coastal artillery. Soviet seamen played a prominent rôle in the defence of Leningrad, due to the proximity of the main Baltic Fleet naval bases. Seamen's shore dress usually consisted of the standard black wool double-breasted *bushlat* pea jacket worn over the traditional blue and white striped cotton shirt. The trousers were black bell-bottoms. On shore, the seamen usually wore Red Army leather boots. The seaman's cap carries the fleet name. The rank insignia up to 1941 was worn on the sleeve of the pea jacket; after 1943 it was moved to the shoulderboards, as in the army. The sleeve insignia indicates the ship's department, or in this case, the branch of the navy to which the seaman is attached. The fabric ammunition belts were traditional for naval infantry, and as much for decorative effect as utility.

C: The Defence of Moscow
C1: Sergeant-Major, Red Army Rifle Force
This sergeant-major (*starshina*) is still wearing the 1941 winter field dress with the more colourful pre-war insignia. The infantry colour was raspberry red, and the greatcoat tab is also accompanied by the sniper badge. He is carrying the older pattern gasmask bag, and is wearing the 1940 period *meshok* rucksack, as is evident from the webbing on his chest. He still wears normal black leather boots. His

weapon is the relatively rare Simonov AVS-36 automatic rifle, one of the few Soviet rifles which was issued with a bayonet scabbard. He is wearing the pre-war *budionovka* wool winter cap.

C2: Red Army Rifleman

This private is wearing the new pattern winter gear introduced in 1941. The most prominent item is the *telogreika*, a quilted khaki winter jacket. These were often issued with similar quilted trousers. Replacing the usual black leather boots are felt *valenki*; these were made from $\frac{1}{4}$in. pressed felt, and were comfortable even in sub-freezing weather. His cap is the new grey 'fish-fur' *shapka-ushanka*, so called as the material it was made from had no relationship with real fur. The *ushanka* had a very square form as it was manufactured in only three sizes, and was therefore worn loose fitting. The soldier is armed with a PPD-34/38 sub-machine gun. He has the usual fabric magazine pouch for a reserve drum on his belt. On his left hip is a grenade pouch; unlike the pre-war pouch, this simple wartime model was open, permitting easier access to the RGD-33 grenade.

Standing next to the rifleman is a Soviet mine-dog. This was a curious Soviet attempt, first begun in the autumn of 1941 outside Moscow, to develop a 'guided' anti-tank mine. The dogs were kept hungry, and trained to crawl under tanks to get their food. In the combat area they were fitted with a special fabric harness which contained 10–12kg of high explosive in four pouches. At the top of the harness was a spring-loaded trigger pin. When the dog crawled under a tank the trigger pin was depressed, setting off a detonator and exploding the charge. The Germans soon learned about this scheme from prisoners, and in sectors where they appeared, dogs in the combat area were shot on sight. German sources claim that the mine dogs were not very effective, apparently because they were trained under diesel-engined Soviet tanks, not petrol-engined German tanks. However, the Soviets continued to use these dogs at least until the battle of Kursk, where Soviet sources claimed that 16 dogs destroyed 12 German tanks.

C3: Tank crewman, 1st Moscow Motorised Rifle Division

This tanker wears the 1941 pattern *shuba* sheepskin coat. Officers were sometimes issued with the

Senior Sergeant Roza Shanina, a sniper credited with 54 kills, wearing the medal of the Order of Glory 2nd and 3rd Class. Her weapon is a Moisin rifle Model 1891/30 with a PU telescopic sight. She is wearing the wartime khaki beret. In the field, she would probably wear the normal two-piece camouflage coverall.

jacket-length *polashubok*, but infantry and enlisted men usually received the longer coat. The helmet is the black fabric type, usually with wool or synthetic fur lining for winter. Tankers were not ordinarily issued *valenki* felt boots, as they were cumbersome for drivers or gunners, who had to be able to use their feet.

D: The Battle for Stalingrad
D1: Red Army Anti-tank Rifleman

This rifleman is equipped with the PTRD 14.5mm anti-tank rifle, capable of penetrating most German tanks up to 1943 if used at very close ranges. The Germans introduced spaced armour on the front of some tanks, like the PzKpfw III, to reduce the effectiveness of these rifles; the spaced

A husband and wife team, ISU-122 tank destroyer commander Guards Lt. Vera Orlova, and the vehicle driver, Guards Lt. Nikolai Orlov. Nikolai is wearing the summer issue *gymnastiorka*, which was often a slightly 'orangeish-buff' colour, while his wife is wearing the darker winter-issue wool *gymnastiorka*. Note that assault gun crew wore the tank insignia on their shoulderboards, not the artillery insignia. This photo was taken on the Third Baltic Front, October 1944, after the couple had participated in three months of fighting.

armour tended to break up the projectile. He is wearing the *plashch-palatka* rain cape/shelter half and a normal *pilotka* sidecap. The PTRD was usually operated by a two-man team, since the long barrel made it very difficult for a single soldier to carry it. The rifle was supplied from a 20-round cartridge pouch, carried either by the rifleman or his No. 2. There was an anti-tank rifle platoon in each rifle battalion, with six PTRD or PTRS rifles.

D2: Red Army Rifleman
By Stalingrad the *telogreika* padded jacket had become common, even in areas where the winters were not particularly severe, as around Stalingrad.

This rifleman wears the *telogreika* without the accompanying padded trousers, wearing the normal khaki *sharovari* instead. He has his *plashch-palatka* cape rolled up, bedroll fashion over his chest. He is wearing the standard Model 1940 steel helmet.

D3: Tank crewman, Red Army
The winter-issue tanker's dress basically consisted of a black leather jacket and trousers worn over the normal winter-issue wool *gymnastiorka* and trousers. From the three triangles on the collar tabs, this tanker is a senior sergeant. Although tankers could carry small arms, as often as not they were not carried outside the tank. As seen in Plate C3, tankers in extremely cold regions could also be issued warmer clothing, such as *shuba* sheepskin coats.

E: Red Army Cossack Cavalry
E1: Captain, Kuban Cossacks
This is an example of Transcaucasus Cossack cavalry at its gaudiest. (However, it should be noted that this is quite simple when compared with the Tsarist period Cossack parade dress!) The dark blue kaftan or *cherkeska* carries decorative silver *gaziri* cartridges. Unlike the rest of the army, the Cossacks wore a shirt with stand-up collar; in the Kuban Cossacks it was red with black piping. This captain, even as late as 1942, wears the pre-war collar tabs, blue with gold trim and a single rectangular bar in red enamel with gold trim. This is completed by the branch symbol of brass crossed sabres. The black *papashka* is worn in traditional fashion, folded at the corners to make it wider at the top than at the bottom. Weapons include the traditional *nagaika* dagger and *shashka* guardless sabre.

E2: Officer, Kuban Cossacks
This shows the Kuban Cossack officer wearing the winter *burka*, a shaggy wool cape. He is wearing the shorter *kubanka* cap, in the Kuban colours of red with a white cross. Over his shoulders is the traditional *bashlyk* scarf, in maroon with black trim.

E3: Lieutenant, Terek Cossacks
This officer is wearing garb more typical of the average Cossack cavalry regiment, basically ident-

patterns, some with two breast pockets, others with a slit pocket over the right breast. Most had a single lap pocket over the right leg.

F2: Red Army Sniper
This female sniper is wearing the standard Soviet issue camouflage coveralls, a two-piece combination in olive green with wavy black splotches. When used by snipers, the hood was usually worn over any headgear. She is armed with a Moisin Model 1891/30 rifle with the PE telescopic sight.

F3: Lieutenant, Red Army Rifle Forces, 1943 Pattern Field Uniform
This officer wears the new 1943 pattern *gymnastiorka* with the stand-up collar and shoulder boards. The infantry shoulder boards were edged in raspberry piping, with a red centre stripe and two stars indicating a lieutenant. He is armed with a PPD-43 sub-machine gun.

G: Operation Bagration
G1: Red Army Scout
The legendary *razvedchiki* usually wore the standard two-piece camouflage combination over normal field dress. The scout troops often preferred the German MP38 or MP40 sub-machine guns, especially when operating behind German lines. This *razvedchik* wears captured German lace-up combat boots, and the normal *pilotka* side cap.

G2: Sergeant, Red Army Traffic Control Branch
One of the more common rôles for women in the frontline areas was traffic control. This young sergeant wears the 1942 pattern khaki skirt, 1943 pattern enlisted men's *gymnastiorka*, and the wartime khaki beret with red star. The traffic control command could be distinguished by the diamond emblem worn on the shoulder with the cyrillic 'R' (resembling Roman 'P') which stood for *rukovodstvo*, or 'control'.

G3: Red Army Sniper
Although snipers usually wore the standard two-piece khaki/black camouflage suit, there was a later medium green suit, known as the *mochalniy*. This was of similar cut to the normal camouflage suit, but had a large number of loops to which simulated fabric foliage was attached and which were ample

Captain A. Pavlyuk, decorated with the Order of Aleksandr Nevsky for his battalion's rôle in combat. The shoulder board is olive-khaki with raspberry edging (infantry) and a single red stripe (junior officer). To the left of the Order of A. Nevsky medal is the Order of the Red Star, and a red wound stripe. Soviet soldiers often wore their awards on combat field dress. The captain's peaked cap is the simple field issue version in overall khaki with no branch of service band or piping.

ical to ordinary Red Army wear; a winter issue officer's *gymnastiorka*, wool *sharovari*, high black riding boots and normal officer's equipment. The only thing that distinguishes him from non-Cossack cavalry is the *kubanka* cap, with the traditional Terek top colours of pale blue with a white cross. He is armed with a PPSh, a very popular weapon with the cavalry.

F: The Battle of Kursk
F1: Tank Crewman, Red Army
The standard uniform for Soviet tankers was this slate-grey or black one-piece coverall, worn over the normal *gymnastiorka* and *sharovari*; this tanker is wearing the new pattern *gymnastiorka* with the stand-up collar. As will be noted, the 1943 shoulderboards were not ordinarily worn on the tanker's coveralls. The coveralls came in different

enough to permit the sniper to add local foliage as well. This sniper is armed with the Moisin Model 1891/30 rifle with the PU sight.

H: The Battle for Berlin

H1: Anti-tank Grenadier, Red Army Rifle Forces

The Red Army captured large stocks of Panzerfaust on their advance west, and also began manufacturing a copy as the RPG-1. These were usually collected by special captured weapons detachments in each regiment, and then issued either to the anti-tank company, or to specific units. This grenadier is in the field dress common at this stage of the war: a padded *telogreika* jacket over the normal winter-issue wool *gymnastiorka* and trousers, with high black boots. The Red Army usually issues it summer weight clothing in May, and so most of the troops in Berlin still had their winter issue wear. The pouch is for the 'banana' clips for the PPSh or PPS-43 sub-machine guns. He wears the winter *ushanka* 'fish fur' cap. The telogreika was not officially covered in dress instructions, though sergeants and officers often attached shoulder boards to it. This grenadier is a sergeant-major (*starshina*) according to his shoulder boards.

H2: Junior Lieutenant, Red Army Artillery

This artillery officer wears the new 1943 pattern

double-breasted greatcoat; this had the new shoulder boards as well as the revised collar-tabs. The background colour of the insignia was an olive-khaki, which stood out from the grey colour of the greatcoat. The buttons on the greatcoat were khaki-brown plastic. He is also wearing the standard Model 1940 helmet, and is armed with a Tokarev pistol. The single star below the artillery's cannon badge on the shoulderboard indicates junior lieutenant.

3: NKVD Internal Security Officer

The NKVD security units generally wore ordinary Red Army gear, but had their own branch of

Carpathian mountains, Fourth Ukrainian Front, winter 1944/45. Colonel Vinogradov, commander of an unidentified Red Army division, meets with Lt. Vinogradov, his son, who commands an artillery battery in his division. Col. Vinogradov wears the senior officers' *papakha* fur hat, and the fur-lined officers' greatcoat. His son wears the normal *ushanka*, and a *shuba* sheepskin coat. The shoulder boards were worn on the greatcoat, but not often on the *shuba*.

service insignia. On occasion, NKVD officers wore the more conspicuous styles of branch insignia as a not very subtle reminder of the power they represented. The officer's peaked cap was made of sky-blue fabric with a red band and red piping. Shoulder boards were blue. He is armed with a Tokarev pistol.

A Kuban Cossack squadron on parade at the end of the war, decked out in *cherkeska*, and with white fur *kubanka*. They are still wearing the pre-war pattern collar tabs.

INDEX

(References to illustrations are shown in **bold**. Plates are shown with caption locators in brackets.)

COMPANION SERIES FROM OSPREY

ESSENTIAL HISTORIES

Concise studies of the motives, methods and repercussions of human conflict, spanning history from ancient times to the present day. Each volume studies one major war or arena of war, providing an indispensable guide to the fighting itself, the people involved, and its lasting impact on the world around it.

CAMPAIGN

Accounts of history's greatest conflicts, detailing the command strategies, tactics, movements and actions of the opposing forces throughout the crucial stages of each campaign. Full-colour battle scenes, 3-dimensional 'bird's-eye views', photographs and battle maps guide the reader through each engagement from its origins to its conclusion.

ORDER OF BATTLE

The greatest battles in history, featuring unit-by-unit examinations of the troops and their movements as well as analysis of the commanders' original objectives and actual achievements. Colour maps including a large fold-out base map, organisational diagrams and photographs help the reader to trace the course of the fighting in unprecedented detail.

ELITE

This series focuses on uniforms, equipment, insignia and unit histories in the same way as Men-at-Arms but in more extended treatments of larger subjects, also including personalities and techniques of warfare.

NEW VANGUARD

The design, development, operation and history of the machinery of warfare through the ages. Photographs, full-colour artwork and cutaway drawings support detailed examinations of the most significant mechanical innovations in the history of human conflict.

WARRIOR

Insights into the daily lives of history's fighting men and women, past and present, detailing their motivation, training, tactics, weaponry and experiences. Meticulously researched narrative and full-colour artwork, photographs, and scenes of battle and daily life provide detailed accounts of the experiences of combatants through the ages.

AIRCRAFT OF THE ACES

Portraits of the elite pilots of the 20th century's major air campaigns, including unique interviews with surviving aces. Unit listings, scale plans and full-colour artwork combine with the best archival photography available to provide a detailed insight into the experience of war in the air.

COMBAT AIRCRAFT

The world's greatest military aircraft and combat units and their crews, examined in detail. Each exploration of the leading technology, men and machines of aviation history is supported by unit listings and other data, artwork, scale plans, and archival photography.